Sex
21 DAY SEX
CHALLENGE

21
**Days of Teasing to Pleasing,
Don't Let One Day Pass**

JOHN PHILLIPS

Introduction

I want to thank you and congratulate you for downloading the book, **"SEX: 21 Day Sex Challenge"**.

This book contains proven ideas on how to take the next 21 days to the next level in your quest for sexual intimacy.

What next, when love alone is not enough for orgasmic sexual pleasure? Do you give into the faulty logic that the once a week missionary sex, is as good as it will ever get? He's probably just as sexually starved as you are. Don't settle for old blind romance when you could easily achieve the perfect O daily.

Researchers say it often takes 21 days to develop a new habit. With this 21 day sex challenge guide, you'll learn to enjoy the lustful messy creative aspects of sex you often fantasize about but never experience. **Remember this is a challenge, don't let one day pass!!**

Thanks again for downloading this book, I hope you enjoy it!

This book is geared towards providing exact and reliable information in regards to the topic and issue covered. The publication is sold on the idea that the publisher is not required to render the accounting, officially permitted, or otherwise, qualified services. If advice is necessary, legal or professional, a practiced individual in the profession should be ordered.

- From a Declaration of Principles which was accepted and approved equally by a Committee of the American Bar Association and a Committee of Publishers and Associations.

The information provided herein is stated to be truthful and consistent, in that any liability, regarding inattention or otherwise, by any usage or abuse of any policies, processes, or directions contained within is the solitary and utter responsibility of the recipient reader. Under no circumstances will any legal respon-

CONTENTS

Day 1- Dirty Talk

Feelings are never complete until they are put into words. You obviously know he loves you, yet you still get that warm fuzzy feeling when he utters the words out loud. It feels even better when he writes it to you. There's a permanence about written words that accords us great comfort and safety. This is because of the conscious thought attached to the sentiment.

A French author says; a woman must be courted before she is kissed. This goes for men too. The renewal of admiration is key. Hearing repeatedly that you're wanted, needed and physically adored pushes you irresistibly towards your man. Why not do the same for him?

Start out the day by leaving a sensual note on the mirror written in red lipstick (or any other color he likes on you). Make it short and memorable. You don't have to be a poet, just be unapologetically raunchy. A few winners you ought to try out.

"Your body looks amazing, even the mirror agrees."

"I'm going to make you beg for it tonight."

"I want to make you cum."

During the day, text him exactly what you want to do and how you're going to do it. A sexy sentence can be the key that starts the engine. Build up his arousal by getting as sweet and explicit as you can. Remember, it's almost impossible to over praise his sexiness.

Men love to feel that they are in our thoughts. Don't just tell him know you love him; let him know you WANT him. I mean really WANT him. If you can arouse him on his office chair, how badly will he want you by that evening?

When he finally comes home, be sure he will be ready for you. Add the sexual tension by whispering a few naughty things you were too afraid to write. I guarantee he will scoop you up before you finish that sentence.

Day 2- Visual Seduction

When was the last time your partner helped or watched you dress? I recently realized that dressing up is equally titillating as undressing in front of him. Lay out that gorgeous dress that makes him go gaga on the bed. On top of it, place the lingerie he bought or picked out for you. The sight of this alone will tease him in anticipation of how it will hug your body in all the right places.

He will hang around till he sees you in it. Now that you have his attention deliver a seductive performance that will leave him wanting more. Do not be in a hurry to strap up your bra, let him join in the action and do it for you. Casually request him to zip up your dress. Then walk out of that door knowing all he will be thinking of is undressing you later.

Foreplay is always timely and should happen continually throughout the day. If your intention wasn't clear in the morning, send him a sexy pic during the day. Let him tease you too. For most ladies, seeing an imprint or the bare outline of his package through his pants or underwear is a major turn on. Be bold and ask for it.

At the end of the day, while his going through his

emails or watching TV, walk by and "accidentally" flash him. Try cleaning braless. Scrub and bounce for him or bend over to dust right in front of him. Leave the room and see if he follows. If he doesn't, take it a notch higher and strip for him. This cannot go unnoticed.

Day 3-Adult Movies

There's something about watching other people writhe in ecstasy together that makes you want to join in the fun. Well, maybe not interrupt their fun but start one of your own. It's exhilarating to bear witness to that kind of intense connection. Adult movies are an excellent way of finding new ideas that you can incorporate in your sexual dalliances. This will help ward off routine sex.

I am inherently straight, but I do get turned on by the sight of two women having sex. I'm also strongly opposed to anal sex (due to the medical implications). This, however, doesn't deter me from feeling a little rumble in the loins at the sight of a woman screaming in pleasure when being anally penetrated.

There are all sorts of things I'd never do in real life, but I've taken pleasure in watching on a smutty streaming service. When you are not daring enough to practice it in real life, why not live through someone else's experience.

There is probably that one thing that you have been hoping he would do to you but he never does it quite right. Instead of an awkward, embarrassing conversation, why not just subtly hint at it by playing him a scene that got it right.

You can make the experience even more salacious by recording an adult movie of your own. Recreate one of the scenes that turned both of you on and ultimately give yourselves into the experience. Fulfill his sexual fantasies and let him quench your desires.

Day 4-Physical Touch

Our hands are said to be the prime laborers of love. We all love to be teased by a sensual touch, whether it's a silly pat on your ass or your breasts being groped. If done right it can lead to voluptuous orgasmic pleasure. Petting is one of the most pleasurable acts of sex. It's the bilateral stimulation of all parts of your body without ending in penile-vaginal penetration.

Challenge yourself and your partner, to achieve this kind of sexual satisfaction. The continuum of sensual touch moves from lesser to greater levels of intimacy.

Affectionate – Sensual – Erotic - Sexual. Slowly build up to the sexual touch without skipping any level. The secret is to find pleasure in the journey as well as the destination.

Subtly initiate it with a nurturing affectionate touch. It could range from a hand on the arm to a 3-second hug when welcoming your man home in the evening. The sensual feel is a bit more luxuriating and is the beginning of sensory pleasure. Think of a lingering caress on the small of the back. It could also be a pleasurable massage of the shoulders using decadent massage oil.

Erotic touch is associated with light petting. It's the arousal play of secondary erogenous zones while fully dressed. Map your way from extra-genital to para-genital and peri-genital areas before arriving at the genital areas. Slowly caress the skin in front of his thorax and the lower abdomen. Move to the scrotal area and its surrounding without touching his man-hood. For the men, feel her inner thighs, rub and lightly spank her ass, fondle her nipples and when she's ready, undress her. Let your hands move fast and slow, here and there complementing each other's movements.

It takes discipline from both of you to reach the sexual stage without having already had an orgasm. You will participate in a game of excitement with physical caressing of all areas completely nude. It can be as simple as kissing or sophisticated nipple-penile contact.

Maximal pleasure will be derived from teasing the genital areas. Gently rub his penile glans, particularly the areas surrounding the frenulum of the foreskin. Guide his hands to stimulate your clitoris and vagina simultaneously. You can add lube to the mix for an explosive experience. Astroglide works best, but some women swear by coconut oil.

Day 5-Oral Sex

It's safe to assume; we've all been kissed. If not I suggest you get that done before reading this guide. We can attest that mouth on mouth contact is pleasurable. If the subtle pressure of lips on lips can stimulate us, what's to be felt when placed against sensitive flesh? We enjoy having our genitals stimulated. To that end, human lips are perfect for the job.

The trick is to do it right. Most men have no clue how to go about it. They go in teeth first and ruin the experience. Guys try these hacks on your girl, and I guarantee she will be begging for more.

Create a comfort zone and make it clear that you are in no rush. If you had messed up before, she's probably still skeptical. Caress, kiss, and touch her before diving down south. Place a pillow under her neck then spread her legs wide for easy access. Start simple by gently licking her inner thighs and area around her labia. Blow a light breeze on her clitoral hood. Take your time teasing her before applying the pressure of your lips.

Slowly gain intensity when she gets into it. Begin with broad tongue strokes with the flattest part of your tongue. Heighten sensation by applying circular motions using the tip of your tongue. Listen to her body. If you notice moans and involuntary movements, you are doing something right.

For the ladies, try these tips to "blow" his mind (pun intended). Pop a mint in your mouth a few minutes before going down on him. It will heighten sensation. Start by slowly licking and kissing his shaft before wrapping your lips around him. Using a broad tongue, slowly lick from under his testicles all the way up to the tip.

Most guys love when you can deep throat, but it's not necessary for amazing oral. Just take in as much as you can. The secret lies in the consistency of your speed and amount of suction. Don't overdo it; you're not trying to give him a hickey. Take a breather in between suctions. Once you've found your groove commit to it. Conveying your genuine enthusiasm will turn him on more than anything.

Day 6- Date Night

Date night is a good way to reconnect with your man. It allows you to talk without interruptions, gaze into each other's eyes, hold hands, laugh and build intimacy with one another. Not all date nights will culminate in mind-blowing sex. Laying the right mood is the backbone to achieving this result.

Go out of your way to be an appealing sight to his sore eyes. Do you recall how self-conscious you were on your first date? Apply the same spirit when picking out the dress you'll wear. I recommend something new. Soak yourself in a scented bath and tease him with a picture of you in it. Make the date a priority and he will too. Engage him in the process of planning it.

The location is essential as it will determine the atmosphere of the date. Stay away from a sports bar; you'll end up sharing his attention with the TV and the crazed fans. Find a place with slow sensual music, good food, and a great ambiance. If your budget is tight make it a home affair with a candle lit dinner and play music in the background.

During the date, pull out all the stops to make him

want you. Remind him why he fell in love with you. Tease him with a bit of foot play under the table. Be daring and rub his junk with your foot. When a sexy song you both love is cued up, sing along to it. My man and I love Hunter Hayes song, wanted. Whenever I start singing; I wanna rock you up, I wanna kiss your lips, he knows I mean what I'm saying.

Find creative ways to be suggestive that you are ready for him. Steer the conversation towards topics that will put him in that frame of mind. Awaken memories of the day you did it behind the bleachers and almost got caught, see if he is up for a similar adventure.

Day 7- Shower Sex

A bathroom romp is one of the most fulfilling experiences you could ever have. Maybe it's the lubricating effect of the water or the fact that you are already in your birthday suit. Either way, once you've engaged in it, you can never have enough.

The first time I had shower sex, it was completely unplanned. The showerhead was loose, and I was afraid the pressure of the water would make it fall. I had just lathered up, so it had to be remedied before I proceeded to shower. I had to call him to tighten it since my hands were too slippery.

When he was done, the sight of his drop dead gorgeous woman, dripping wet turned him on. We both seized the opportunity and made it a ritual. If you have a similar problem with your showerhead, don't let it go to waste. If not create an excuse for him to find his way in the shower while you are nude and wet. Deliberately forget your towel in the bedroom and ask him to bring it to you.

When he stares longingly, write a naughty message on the misty shower glass with your finger. It could be as simple as, "you want it, come get it." If you have no shower glass saying the words out loud will do just fine!

Once his in, make the experience sensual and playful. Tease him by lathering every inch of his body with your bare hands paying extra attention to his shaft. Guide him to do the same to you. Let him scrub the dirt off you as slowly as he can. Let him press you on the shower door; comfort is overrated at this point.

Day 8 – Role-playing

Role-play is both a finely choreographed dance and an aphrodisiac. It requires you to fully become someone else and not just in bed but in the moments leading to it. If you want to yield significant results, commit to a character the whole day.

Make it a teamwork effort. Start by picking out two characters for both of you. If you enjoy the plot of Game of thrones, pick any two lovers that intrigue you. Is he turned on, by the gorgeous, Khaleesi? Have you taken a liking to the well-built muscular Khal Drogo? Choose characters and a context that works for you. Think in the lines of Romeo and Juliet if you're a hopeless romantic.

You don't have to go for a full makeover, to physically pass as the character you've chosen. Just choose one dominant feature about the character and make it your own. Think of the luscious long white hair of Khaleesi or the long braided ponytail of Khal Drogo. Get a wig that resembles this and put it on. Do a bit of recon to get a better background of your character.

You can start of his day by addressing him in the tone that Khaleesi would have addressed her Khal. Spark up a stimulating conversation with him during the day in the context of your fantasy. Make it as believable as you possibly can.

Reiterate the same words they exchanged. Use the same pet names they used. Refer to your man as your sun and stars when he calls you the moon of his life. Be sure to find words which will captivate your partner. If you can stimulate his mind, then you'll surely intrigue his body. A few examples in this context would be:

"You're the moon of my life; that's all I know, and I need to know and if this is a dream I will kill the man who tries to wake me."

"When the sun rises in the west and sets in the east. When the mountains blow in the wind like leaves. Then you shall return to me my sun and stars."

Day 9- Masturbation

Masturbating is necessary to figure out what feels best to you. It will, in turn, help you to communicate better with your partner. It's been documented that most women have their first orgasm from masturbating. This breaks an absolute barrier, so to speak, particularly in female sexuality. You become more in tune with your body. It ultimately leads to better sex.

If you're afraid of being caught, you can do it in the shower alone. Try pointing the showerhead on your V if it's portable. The pressure of the water will tease you. Work your way up to watching porn as you pad your lily.

Contrary to popular belief, masturbation does not have to be a solitary vice. It can be enjoyed in the company of your partner. If you're not brave enough to do it in front of him, start by sending him a pre-recorded video. His response will boost your confidence to do it while he's physically there.

Make it more fun by loosely tying his hands together. Use one of his ties to do this; silk works best. Slowly take off your clothes and throw them his way. Let him watch without touching. Ask him what he wants to see you do.

Don't rush the experience. Let out that startling moan with no inhibitions when it feels right. Losing yourself in the pleasure will make your man bust out of that tie and join you. Watch him jerk off too. Remember, sex works best with a give and take dynamic.

Day 10- Quickie

A spontaneous hump and dash is incredibly sexy. The adrenaline that courses through your body heightens the sensation, especially if you're in a not so private area. You've probably had those fantasies where he takes you in the elevator and humps your brains out before anyone else gets in. Or maybe you've thought of sneaking in a quick romp in his office a few minutes before a major meeting.

If so, you're not alone; we've all had them. The problem is that the fantasies never seem to materialize. We often have an unrealistic flawless execution of events in our fantasies that could never match up to reality. We assume that your man can read your mind when you wink at him in the elevator like you did in your fantasy. Or maybe expect when you show up in his office braless he will get the gist, clear his desk and take you there and then.

A planned quickie is just as fun as those natural ones you've dreamt of regularly. Think of it as a slow pursuit with a quick end. Start out by sharing one of your well-thought-out fantasies. Tell your man in detail what went where for how long and of course how it felt without leaving anything out. He might surprise you and share his fantasies as well.

Incorporate both your fantasies when planning for a real life quickie. Choose a location that is somewhat comfortable yet still adventurous. I propose car sex while in traffic or joining the mile high club on your next flight.

Talk about the things you plan on doing to him. Tease him with a few naughty photos. Keep in mind that you won't have time for a lot of foreplay and slow lovemaking. It's best to arrive ready to go! If you don't get it right the first time, try and try again.

Day 11- Sex Toys

Sex toys are one of the most controversial sexual vices in this generation. I like to think that in sex, what you like is what you like. If something interests you, you shouldn't hold back. Why conform to societal judgmental views when your partner is equally willing to explore "weird" stuff with you? Trying new things is a wonderful way to expand and spice up the sex you're having.

When used alone, they allow you to discover ways of having better orgasms. Some women have confessed to having had their G-spot aroused for the first time while using a toy. This spot is an area that is not just pleasurable but wildly excitable. Those who mention this, place it in the anterior vaginal wall.

Since his shaft is attached to his body, there's a limit to the type of movements and strokes it can make. With a toy you are in control of everything, how deep, which direction, what intensity and even the size. The confidence gained from controlling your sexuality is important in fostering sex positive feelings.

By now you're aware of what works for you and what doesn't. Knowing what you like can lead you to a toy that best serves that purpose. Choose a toy that will bring immense pleasure to both you and your partner. They can be super fun and provide a unique sexual experience every time.

A sex toy should complement your sexual relationship, not replace him. As exciting as they are, a toy will not talk, touch and love you the way he does. Find a healthy balance of the two by including him in the fun.

Day 12- Exercise

Sex might just be the most if not only pleasurable workout. Let's face it; if we could look good and keep fit minus the physical torture that is exercise, we would never workout. If you exercise regularly, (I mean the real kind) you can attest that it not only made you more flexible but also built your endurance. It will ultimately lead to better sex. You can almost give those toys a run for their money in intensity and speed.

Most of us can barely carve out any time for exercise. You're juggling careers, businesses, relationships and "other" obligations. Understandably, most days are packed. If you can't hack a daily workout routine, start by exercising once a week. Choose a day you can do it together with your man

The cool thing is that it doesn't have to be a long and drawn workout. A 10 to 15-minute quickie is just enough to get your heart rate up and break a sweat. On those days you can do it together, make it a sexy affair.

Look for a comfortable yet still appealing exercise gear. The tighter it is, the better. For your warm up tease your man with provocative stretches. Continue the show with jumping jacks while facing his way. Engage him by asking him to count as you jump up and down. Next, let him spot you as you do squats.

If this is not your cup of tea, try a dancing workout video. Choose one with a lot of provocative styles. If there's some twerking involved, I approve!

Day 13- Kitchen Sex

The power of a culinary delight cannot be underestimated. Kitchen sex does not have to be a quick hump on the kitchen island when you accidentally bump into each other while reaching for the ketchup. You can make it a long, exciting experience.

Invite him to keep you company as you prepare dinner. Think of an easy recipe that you can both contribute to making. Use all the tools at your disposal to tease him. Wear the sexiest apron you can find. If it has something naughty written on it the closer, you'll be to getting laid.

Engage him with something light like cutting onions or better yet turning on the heater. You want his attention to be on you and not on the food you're preparing. When you bend over to open the oven, direct your bum in his direction. If he is in the way of something you want, don't ask him to pass it. Go ahead and "accidentally" graze him with your boob as you reach for it. Let him taste the food from the palm of your hand or lick your finger if it's a creamy dessert.

Ingeniously drop in seductive hints in the conversation. One you can try out is.

"Come feel this beefy steak, is it thick enough?"

After you've placed the food in the oven, be more aggressive. Smear something on your apron to find an excuse to take your top off.

Day 14- Rewards/gifts

On my anniversary, I gave my man four sex coupons. They were to be redeemed anytime and anyplace he wanted, within the course of that month. At the time it felt like a silly gift to lighten the mood. He, of course, knew all he had to do was get me horny and I would comply, with or without the coupons.

I grossly underestimated the effect it would have on our relationship. I had honestly expected us to laugh and forget about it. My guy surprised me when he cashed in all his chips within a span of a week. I kid you not; it was the best week of my life.

Later on, he explained why that particular gift intrigued him. At a subconscious level, the coupons reassured him, that I'm fully his and I enjoy being his. From that experience, we learned to ask for it when we wanted it.

Gifts of any kind will bring you closer to your partner. Do not wait for a holiday to buy him that watch his been eyeing. Guys don't wait for Valentine's Day to bring her that beautiful bouquet of flowers and chocolate. Make it a habit to continually show your partner gratitude through gifts.

It does not have to be exorbitant $5,000 shopping sprees but if you can afford it spend it. Aim at pulling his heartstrings. When you're in the mood for something naughtier, present yourself to him in nothing but a big bow. After all, you are the greatest gift in his life.

Day 15- Slow Sex

Slow sex deepens intimacy. It transcends beyond the mechanical function or even the biological urge of sexual intercourse. It's perhaps the highest level of lovemaking. You are acutely aware of his breath, his essence and his untamed desire for you in each moment. Its only fault is the time it consumes.

Our plates are already full, who has time to gaze into someone else's eyes? In the face of time-pressure, our instinct is to react straight away. So we start doing and that doing becomes more and more lackluster as we accord less and less time. Good things come to those who are patient.

Clear your schedule on a Sunday afternoon and spend quality with him. Remember you have the whole day to fool around so take your time. Let the foreplay drag on an on till you can't hold it any longer. It should be done with a sense of exploration rather than urgency. Surrender to each other in lust and trust. Change location from the bedroom to the living room. When you feel dirty, take it to the bathroom and hump some more. When hunger sets in, order take-out, and then fool around some more.

Day 16- Literature & Art

We are emotional beings with delicate souls. Feelings gush out of us like a waterfall whenever we experience something moving. We laugh at a hilarious comedy, cuddle when watching a romantic movie and cry when we someone in pain. We are wired to react when we feel.

Art is solely created for us to get in touch with our feelings. Think of the Beyonce concert you attended, how did the love songs make you feel? I bet you it put in you in the right mood for a sexy romp with your man. Recreate that feeling by attending a tour of your favorite musician with him.

Drag him along to a reading of a romantic novel. As the imagery is conjured up in your mind be sure his thinking of the same too. Tease by reading one of the erotic scenes out loud when it's just the two of you. Art is best appreciated when it's shared.

Day 17-Morning Glory

Morning sex is like having the utmost pleasure of eating chocolate cake before the break of day with relaxing breakfast ahead. We are often exhausted at night and fail to respond accordingly to our partner's advances. You've probably pretended to be deep asleep when he tried to wake you for a midnight grind.

For most of us, when the alarm clock rings and bars out our ears may not be a welcome sound. However, when it opens with a relishing morning sex, it makes things all the more fantastic and energetic the whole day.

The best taste of lust is in the morning when your mind and soul are at a primal state. To stay safe, I suggest you keep condoms at arm's length so that you do not have to search the room. Brush your teeth the night before and keep a few chewing gums around to refresh your breath.

Morning sex helps to ensure fat loss. Sex hormones flickers within the body, which if given a chance will assist in burning fat early in the day. It's also said that morning sex makes you feel upbeat and prepares your body for a stronger immune system.

Day 18- Hotel Sex

There's a certain je ne sais quoi attributed to hotel sex that makes it naughtier, hotter and leaves you gasping for breath. Imagine how great sex was on your honeymoon. I bet it was on fire!

Book the room earlier in the day and arrive at separate times. Make it more scandalous by pretending to be an escort or having an affair. Call ahead and make sure the room has a Jacuzzi or a hot tub for a nice bubble bath. Let them avail you with chilled champagne and strawberries.

Live out those incredibly juicy hotel fantasies to completion. Take advantage of someone else catering to your needs and completely let yourself go.

Day 19-Outdoor Sex

Sexual awakening is found on beaches and picnics. There's no better feeling than being one with nature and your man. Rainy or sunny, both kinds of weather will do just fine. The adventure is in the open space; the weather cannot take away from the experience.

Like all other challenges research and planning takes the pressure off it. Find a suitable location that is not so crowded yet romantic for your outdoor getaway. A well, manicured green park is preferable for a picnic. Strap on a sexy dress that can easily come off and on.

Beach sex is just inherently romantic. It can help us to get in the mood. The right atmosphere can do wonders for our libido. That said, it's best to lay a towel down on the sand. You don't want it getting into tricky areas. Stick to getting busy on land. Salt water can dry out the skin in your nether regions.

Head on the beach at a time you are sure you'll have a perfect view of the rise and tides of the ocean. Carrying along an iPod for beautiful music is an added advantage. Setting the mood will not be hard. You'll be among beautiful sights that will captivate you to make lasting memories.

Day 20- New Sex-position

The logistical nightmare of trying a new sexual position can scare you to stick to the basics. You've probably read articles touting top tips for new sex position guaranteed to change the game. You tried, failed and gave up. Don't be disheartened; real sex affords you the freedom to get it wrong.

Setting aside expectations, even just occasionally, gives us freedom to be creative. Make sure you create a safe space for experimentation by being comfortable. You might have started by trying out a sophisticated position and in the process ended up discovering a new one. Go with the flow and welcome the experience.

Complement reading with visual aids when you're not so sure what's supposed to go where. Involve him in the research to put you in sync when you're trying it out. Practice ongoing active consent while performing the deed.

What feels great to you might be hurting him. You can do this verbally with some sexy whispering or dirty talk.

"Do you like it when I squeeze your nipples? Do you want me to do it harder?"

You can also physically do this by looking for certain cues. If your man is holding your eye contact, kissing you back and pulling you closer, proceed. When he withdraws from touch or his muscles, suddenly become stiff, check in with him.

Make sure your partner knows that if he wants to stop, that desire will be respected and you will proceed with care. By doing this, you're creating a space in which experimentation can flourish.

Day 21-Enhanced Performance

Sex drugs, despite their artificial connotation, are massive messengers of "supernatural" natural feelings. It makes everything all the more beautiful for what it inherently is. It's a great way of allowing yourself to let loose and wild with your man completely.

If he has a problem getting it up, try Viagra. Be careful not to make him feel insecure. Get an enthusiastic consent from him before daring to proceed. When you're both on the same page, go ahead and research about your drug of choice.

A checklist of the questions to ask include:

Is it FDA approved?

Does it have any side effects?

Are we suitable candidates for use?

How long do its effects last?

How much should I take?

Is it contraindicated with alcohol or any other drug I'm taking?

After you are completely sure it's safe, proceed to have the time of your life. Do it in a controlled environment, preferably at home.

Conclusion

Thank you again for downloading this book!

I hope this book was able to help you to reach the 21-Day Sex Challenge

Finally, if you enjoyed this book, then I'd like to ask you for a favor, would you be kind enough to leave a review for this book on Amazon? It'd be greatly appreciated!

Thank you and good luck!

Made in the USA
Columbia, SC
10 September 2019